D1500522

THE
ESTABLISHED
Heart

THE ESTABLISHED HEART

ISBN 0-89274-068-X

Unless otherwise stated, all Scripture quotations are taken from *The King James Version* and *The Amplified Version* of the Bible.

Jerry Savelle Ministries Int'l.
P. O. Box 748
Crowley, TX 76036

JERRY SAVELLE

THE
ESTABLISHED
Heart

❦ ❦ ❦

CONTENTS

CHAPTER
1

The
Established
HEART
&
The
Troubled
HEART

❦ ❦ ❦

Praise ye the Lord. Blessed is the man that feareth the Lord, that delighteth greatly in his commandments. His seed shall be mighty upon the earth: the generation of the upright shall be blessed. Wealth and riches shall be in his house: and his righteousness endureth for ever. Unto the upright there ariseth light in the darkness: he is gracious, and full of compassion, and righteous. A good man sheweth favour, and lendeth: he will guide his affairs with discretion. Surely he shall not be moved for ever: the righteous shall be in everlasting remembrance. He shall not be afraid of evil tidings: his heart is fixed, trusting in the Lord. His heart is established, he shall not be afraid, until he see his desire upon his enemies. Psalm 112:1-8

The Scriptures we will be using specifically in this study are found in verse 7 and 8. Let's look at them again. I want you to pay close attention to what the Psalmist is saying here. *He shall not be afraid of evil tidings: his heart is fixed, trusting in the Lord. His heart is established, he shall not be afraid, until he see his desire upon his enemies.*

Psalm 112 is the description of a man who has his heart established in God's Word. He is not afraid of evil tidings; he is not afraid of bad news; he is not moved by contradictory evidence; he is not moved by the woes and cares and pressures of this world. His heart is fixed and settled, trusting in the Lord.

The times in which we live today offer us ample opportunity to be troubled, to be afraid, to be easily shaken by bad news. The newscasts are filled with it. You can focus your attention on the problems in the world. You can look at the trouble, listen to the bad news, and talk about it to other people; but you are only magnifying the works of the devil. The Bible says that where sin abounds, grace does much more abound (Romans 5:20). Today, we are in the perfect position to have the grace of God manifested at its absolute greatest.

You must realize one very important fact: The Believer can live today in the midst of all the turmoil and the pressures in the world without being shaken by them. You can live with your heart established, trusting in the Lord, and not be afraid of anything Satan can bring upon the earth.

The sixth verse of Psalm 112 says, *Surely he shall not be moved forever.* Has this been your confession for the last six months of your Christian life? Verse 7 says, *He shall not be afraid of evil tidings.* Can you declare that during the last six months of your Christian life, you have not been afraid of evil tidings? If you cannot, then your heart is not established. If you are being troubled over the happenings in the world - if you are afraid and shaken and unstable over the world situation - then you can be sure that your heart

17

is not established. I do not mention this to put you under condemnation. My purpose is to strike your thinking and bring these things to your attention so that you can do something about them.

If you want to be like the man described in the 112th Psalm, then you must reach the point where you are not moved by anything - not by what you hear or by what you see or by what you feel. The established heart is settled and fixed in the Word of the Living God. The established heart knows that in every situation, God is more than enough and He will meet his every need according to His riches in glory by Christ Jesus. I am convinced that this is the intention of the Father God for every Believer.

The established heart trusts in the Lord. If you expect to trust in the Lord, you must trust His Word because God and His Word are one and the same. You will never be able to have your heart established except by the Word of God. It takes God's Word to get the job done.

We have read what the Psalmist has to say about the established heart. Now let's see what Jesus taught. In Matthew 24, Jesus was teaching His disciples about the signs of His returning and of the end of the world. I must caution you not to read these Scriptures religiously. If you do, you will miss what the Spirit of God instructed Jesus to say. If you read them religiously, you will see only woes and problems and cares; you will think that we are to be tortured and doomed and live in destruction. The things Jesus mentions here have a tendency to shake people. They tend to make one's heart afraid. However, you must keep in mind that Jesus always preaches good news, not bad news. The Bible tells us that Jesus is the author and the finisher of faith, not fear (Hebrews 12:2). Every sermon Jesus preached was delivered under the anointing of the Holy Spirit and was designed to inspire and create faith in the hearts of the hearers.

In Matthew 24, Jesus was teaching that even in the midst of the worst onslaught of Satan, we are not to be troubled; we are to live above the beggarly elements of the world; we are to have our hearts established, not afraid of evil tidings; and we are to be moving on in the things of God.

Notice Jesus' words in Matthew 24:4. His disciples have asked Him a legitimate question. What shall be the sign of thy coming and of the end of the world ? His first reply was *Take heed that no man deceive you.* Why would He make such a statement first? Because He realizes that in the midst of the signs of His returning and of the end of the world, there will be many things preached that are not the Gospel. It is the responsibility of each Believer to discern the difference between the truth of the Gospel and false teaching.

The five-fold ministry has been sent to preach the Word in order that the Body of Christ be perfected (Ephesians 4:11-12). The minister of God cannot perfect you; all he can do is preach the Word. It is up to YOU, the individual Believer, to bring about the perfection. It is what YOU do with the Word that will bring perfection in your life.

Another thing I want you to notice from the 24th Chapter of Matthew is verse 6; *And ye shall hear of wars and rumours of wars: see that ye be not troubled. . .* Jesus is listing all the things that must come to pass before He returns - wars and rumours of wars, nation rising against nation, famines, pestilence, earthquakes, etc. However, in the midst of this, He makes one very outstanding statement: *SEE THAT YE BE NOT TROUBLED*. Jesus did not waste words. Every word He spoke was anointed of God and inspired by the Holy Spirit. If He says, *SEE THAT YOU BE NOT TROUBLED*, then there must be a way for us to live in the midst of turmoil and not be troubled by it.

Notice verse 14; *And this gospel of the kingdom shall be preached in all the world for a witness unto all nations; and then shall the end come.* The word *GOSPEL* means *GOOD NEWS*. Jesus is saying that even in the midst of bad news and hard times, somebody will be standing and proclaiming the Good News of the Gospel. What is good news in hard times? That there is a way out, that God is our Source

21

of supply, that He meets *ALL* our needs according to His riches in glory by Christ Jesus. The witness will be the preaching of the Good News. When we have preached all the Good News we possibly can, *THEN* the end will come, not until.

There is a way to live in the earth at this time without being afraid or being tossed to and fro. You can get full of the Word of God and become established, settled, fixed, trusting in the Lord, and not be moved for ever. The Apostle Paul is the perfect example of a man with an established heart. His writings in the 8th Chapter of Romans bear out what both the Psalmist and Jesus have said.

Romans 8:31-39 is the confession of a Believer whose heart is established in God's Word. By the time Paul wrote these words, he had been through just about everything hell could throw his way. Why? Because of the abundance of revelations he had received. Jesus taught in the 4th Chapter of Mark that when the seed of the Word is sown in your heart, Satan comes immediately to take it away. Paul was dangerous to Satan because he was full of the revelation of the New Testament which Jesus had given him. Consequently, Satan tried every way he could to stop Paul and defeat him. But the Apostle Paul did not give in; he stood fast! He proved that these things would work. He proved that the authority of the Believer is to put on the whole armor of God, take the shield of faith and quench ALL the fiery darts of the wicked !

The Apostle Paul lived through more than enough calamities for one lifetime, and still he wrote, *Who shall separate us from the love of Christ? shall tribulation, or distress, or persecution, or famine or nakedness, or peril, or sword ?...Nay, in all these things we are more than conquerors through him that loved us. For I am persuaded, that neither death, nor life, nor angels...nor any other creature, shall be able to separate us from the love of God, which is in Christ Jesus our Lord* (Romans 8:35, 37-39).

Find out what the Apostle Paul learned about the New Testament and you, too, can stand in the midst of Satan, demons, sickness, disease, and even death itself and say, "I am persuaded that *NOTHING* can separate me from the love of Christ. I am *MORE THAN A CONQUEROR* in all these things!" Paul was established in the Word and it made him able to stand victoriously, more than a conqueror!

Jesus gives a clear illustration of the established heart. In Matthew 7:24-27, He describes two men who heard the Word. One man heard the Word and acted on it. He was established in the Word. As Jesus said, *I will liken him unto a wise man, which built his house upon a rock.* The rock is the Word of God. This man built his house and laid his foundation on the rock of the Word. Jesus said that when the flood came, that man's house would not be shaken; it would not be destroyed. Why? Because his foundation was on the Word and you cannot shake a man whose heart is established in God's Word.

The second man Jesus described also heard the Word, but he did not act on it. Jesus likened him to a *FOOLISH MAN,*

WHICH BUILT HIS HOUSE UPON THE SAND. Luke's account of this says, *But he that heareth, and doeth not, is like a man that without a foundation built a house upon the earth.* . . The man that only hears the Word is without a foundation. Ask any builder and he will tell you that a house is only as good as its foundation. If the foundation is weak, the house is weak. The foolish man's house was without a foundation and he could not expect to stand against the storms and floods of life.

Luke 6 says that the wise man "digged deep" in the rock and laid his foundation. Have you ever tried to dig into a rock? It isn't easy, but it can be done. I am not implying that living by faith and getting your heart established in God's Word is easy. Satan will not simply lay down and let you get founded in the Word; he will do his best to stop it. But don't be discouraged. The more Word you get into your spirit, the stronger you will grow. It is to your advantage to become settled and fixed on the Word so that the floods and storms of life will not shake you.

Another example of a man whose heart is established is found in Mark 5:21-43. Jairus, the ruler of the synagogue, came to Jesus and asked Him to heal his little daughter. In verse 23, Jairus makes a statement of faith: *I pray thee, come and lay thy hands on her, that she may be healed; and she shall live.* Jairus believed in his heart that when Jesus laid His hands on that little girl, she would be healed and live. He made his statement of faith to Jesus, and Jesus started to follow him to his house. Then the little woman with the issue of blood caught Jesus' attention. She, too, had made a faith demand upon His ability.

Jesus stopped to minister to the little woman and while He was attending to her, some messengers came to Jairus and said, *Thy daughter is dead: why troublest thou the Master any further?* You see, Jairus had made his statement of faith and Satan came immediately to steal away the Word. The pressure was on. Did Jairus change his confession? Did he say, "I don't understand why it didn't work for me?" This is a crucial point where many people miss

26

out on the blessings of God. We say what we believe we pray, "Father, in the name of Jesus, I believe I receive according to Mark 11:24 and my faith says it's mine now." Then circumstances arise and try to prove that there is no way for us to receive what we are believing for. At this point, you must either talk the Word or keep your mouth shut. If you do not talk the Word, then whatever you do say will negate the prayer you prayed. In my own experience, there have been times when I have said absolutely nothing and put Satan on the run as quickly as I do when I talk the Word. This is what happened with Jairus. He did not open his mouth.

Notice what Jesus said in verse 36. *As soon as Jesus heard the word that was spoken, he saith unto the ruler of the synagogue, Be not afraid, only believe.* Jesus was exhorting Jairus to be like the man in Psalm 112, not afraid of evil tidings but trusting in Him to follow up on what he is believing for. The moment Jesus heard that negative evil report, He turned to Jairus and said, *Be not afraid, only believe.* After much time spent meditating on this incident, I can almost see the expression on Jairus' face. He was the ruler of the synagogue. The religious people of that day did not think very highly of Jesus and by going to Jesus, Jairus laid his job on the line. He had overlooked the religious leaders around him and had publicly thrown himself at Jesus' feet.

After the messengers came with bad news, the circumstances looked as if there was total defeat. But the bad news did not alarm Jesus. He was not shaken by it. You will notice in Jesus' earth walk that He was never in a hurry. You will never catch Jesus making a negative confession. He did not turn to Jairus and say, "Well, we tried; but some of us get it and some of us don't." No, the moment He heard the evil report, He exhorted Jairus to *BE NOT AFRAID*. One translation says, *And He turned to Jairus and said, Don't open your mouth, just keep believing. I'll take care of this.* When Jesus finished ministering to the little woman, He followed Jairus to his house and did just what Jairus was believing Him for. In the midst of all the turmoil that had broken out, Jesus walked in confidently, grabbed that little girl by the hand, and said, *Damsel, I say unto thee, arise.* The whole time, Jairus was still holding fast to what he believed. His heart was established in what he believed. He was trusting in the Lord.

Can you see the part that the established heart plays in the life of a Believer? The reason so many Christians are being robbed of the blessings of God is because they have failed to get God's Word into their hearts and get their hearts established in it. If you pray according to God's Word and follow the instructions outlined there, you WILL get results. If you miss it, then it is your fault, not God's.

I am convinced from studying God's Word that He has no pleasure in weak and feeble children. He loves them; He will care for them; He will protect them; but He has no pleasure in them. A weak and feeble Christian is one that is ignorant of his covenant with God. It is not pleasing to God when His children do not know the things He has provided for them in Christ.

If a man will put God's Word first place in his life and exalt it above everything else, then that Word will create the image of the Lord Jesus Christ in that man's heart and he can expect to receive the results in his own life which Jesus had when He walked the earth nearly 2,000 years ago. You can read through the Gospels and see that Jesus never missed it! He never failed. He never once was defeated. He was never at a point where He could not overcome with the things God had given Him. Well, praise God, the Believer is equipped with the same things Jesus had in His earthly ministry!

CHAPTER
2

Seven Major Revelations *Every Believer Should Know*

❧ ❧ ❧

There are seven major revelations from God's Word in which every Believer should be established. Once you become established in these areas, you will be in a strong position to not be moved by the circumstances surrounding you. You will be as Jesus said in Matthew 24, untroubled in the midst of all Satan can throw your way.

The Apostle Paul was established in these revelations. The Lord Jesus Christ had personally revealed these things to him. Paul understood the authority of the Believer, the inheritance of the saints, who we are in Christ, and what we have in Christ. These revelations were a vital part of his life; consequently, Paul could stand in the face of sickness, disease, shipwreck, demons - in the face of hell itself - and say, "I am persuaded that none of these can separate me from the love of Christ. I am more than a conqueror in all these things."

These seven revelations should become so vitally real to you as a Believer that you stand unaffected, regardless of what is happening in the world around you. This is what Jesus was praying when He said, *Father, thy will be done on earth as it is in heaven.* Heaven is not affected by the things on earth, and Jesus was implying that we should have a part of heaven where we are now. We should be able to live like heaven here on earth. We are to be governing the circumstances around us with the Word of the Living God. If your circumstances do not line up with the Word of God, take the Word and change them!

With God's Word firmly established in your heart, you will be like the man in Psalm 112; your heart will be fixed; you will be trusting in the Lord and completely unshaken by evil tidings. The moment a problem arises, these revelations from God's Word will be activated inside you and they will flow out your mouth. The words you speak will be according to God's Word and the problem before you will have to desist in its maneuvers against you. No weapon formed against you shall prosper!

REVELATION #1
REALITY OF REDEMPTION

The first revelation you must become established in is the truth of your redemption in Christ - what it means to you as a Believer. Hebrews 9:11-14 tells of the work Jesus did in obtaining our redemption with His blood. Verse 12 says, ...*but by his own blood he entered in once into the holy place, having obtained eternal redemption for us.*

There are three important facts about the redemptive work of Christ which every Believer should know!

1. **OUR REDEMPTION HAS AL-READY BEEN OBTAINED FOR US.** Hebrews 9:12 which we just quoted uses the past tense, **HAVING OBTAINED**.

2. **OUR REDEMPTION IS AN ETERNAL REDEMPTION**. If it is an eternal redemption, then Satan is eternally defeated!

Sin and Satan should not be lord over you in any way whatsoever!

3. **OUR REDEMPTION IS OPERATIVE NOW.** You do not have to wait until Heaven to enjoy the benefits of your redemption. It is available right now!

The Apostle Paul wrote some very important things about our redemption in Ephesians 1:3-9. Verse 7 says, *In whom we have redemption through his blood...* Our redemption is a settled fact.

Jesus was the final sacrifice under the Abrahamic Covenant. He was the Lamb of God, offered up on the altar of the cross by the High Priest. Never again would men

36

have to offer the blood of bulls and goats as the sacrifice for sin. Jesus paid the price once and for all, purchasing our eternal redemption!

When the Father God proclaimed Him King of Heaven and earth, Jesus returned to earth and said to His disciples, *All power is given unto me in heaven and in earth* (Matthew 28:18). What did He do with this power? Did He take it back with Him to Heaven? No, He said, *Go ye therefore into all the world in My Name and do these things...* Jesus took the power given Him and placed it in the hands of man. He then ascended into Heaven and took His position at the right hand of the Father. He is seated there, fully expecting His enemies to be made His footstool.

God gave us the authority that Jesus took from Satan. It is now our responsibility to keep Satan under our feet. You should not allow Satan to run your home. You should not allow him to be lord over your finances and over the affairs of your life. Once you become established in your redemption - the redemption that Jesus obtained for you at a precious price - you will refuse to let Satan have any dominion over you whatsoever!

Let's look at Galatians 3:13,14 to see just exactly what our redemption involves. You should know this Scripture by heart. *Christ hath redeemed us from the curse of the law, being made a curse for us: for it is written, Cursed is every one that hangeth on a tree: That the blessing of Abraham might come on the Gentiles through Jesus Christ; that we might receive the promise of the Spirit through faith.* YOU ARE REDEEMED FROM THE CURSE OF THE LAW! Read the 28th Chapter of Deuteronomy from verse 15, and you will see the things involved in this curse. It lists every sickness, every disease, every plague, every calamity known to mankind. Verse 61 even says, *Also every sickness, and every plague, which is not written in the book of this law...* That covers everything from hangnails to tuberculosis !

Galatians 3:29 tells what our redemption purchased. *If ye be Christ's, then are ye Abraham's seed, and heirs according to the promise.* Deuteronomy 28:1-14 outlines all the blessings of Abraham. Study these and get them fixed in your spirit. You will realize that you have a covenant with God, signed in the blood of Jesus. Jesus is the surety of that covenant. It will work for you now! YOU HAVE A LEGAL RIGHT TO BE BLESSED BY GOD. Deuteronomy 28:7 says that the Lord will bless all that you set your hand to. If your enemy comes against you one way, God will cause him to flee seven ways! God said that He would make you the head and not the tail - that you will be above only and you shall not be beneath!

How does a reality of your redemption in Christ affect the things happening around you right now? Once you get established and fixed in the reality of your redemption, you will realize your authority as a Believer; you will realize that you do not have to stand for anything Satan throws your way. Ephesians 1:22 says that God has put ALL things under Jesus' feet. Where are the feet? On the Body, and the Believers make up His Body. All principality and power has been placed under His feet; therefore, all principality and power has been placed under YOU. You have an inheritance as a saint, and your redemption and authority are a part of this inheritance.

You are redeemed and the Bible says, *LET THE REDEEMED OF THE LORD SAY SO.* Dare to say what your redemption means in your life. Jesus paid a precious price for it! I absolutely refuse to lay down under the onslaught of Satan and let him think he is triumphant over me after what Jesus Christ did at Calvary to buy my freedom. The Son has made me free and I am free indeed ! Your redemption is operative now. Become established in it.

REVELATION #2
REALITY OF THE NEW BIRTH

Therefore, if any man be in Christ, he is a new creature: old things are passed away; behold, all things are become new. And all things are of God... (2 Corinthians 5:17-18). We are new creations. The literal Greek says we are A NEW SPECIES

OF BEING THAT NEVER EXISTED BEFORE. This is what you become when you make Jesus your Lord. Quit dwelling on that old man. He died the death of the cross and a new man took his place - a new man created in the likeness of God.

The new creation has access to the ability of God. Second Peter 1:4 says that we have been made partakers of the divine nature of God. The nature of God is eternal life, and the actual life of God was imparted to your spirit at the New Birth. Jesus said in John 10:10, ...*I am come that they might have life, and that they might have it more abundantly*. His Life is the Source of our ability. We are not limited by the things of this earth. We are not limited to natural, human resources. We are partakers of God's divine nature. Therefore, we have access to His ability, to His wisdom, to His anointing, to His power, to His love, and to His faith. His divine nature takes into account all the attributes of God and we are partakers of that nature! When this becomes a reality in your spirit, you will no longer see yourself from a carnal viewpoint. You will see yourself as Ephesians 2:10, *For we are his work-manship, created in Christ Jesus unto good works, which God hath before or-dained that we should walk in them.* This is the way God sees you. A revelation of the New Birth in your spirit will cause these things to become a reality to you and you will act accordingly.

Many Christians today are being robbed of the blessings of God simply because they are not established in the New Birth. Through ignorance, they have allowed Satan to bring up to them things they did before they accepted Jesus. He keeps them living in condemnation, thinking that God does not love them. Without a revelation of the New Birth in your spirit, Satan will keep you in the arena of that old creation, robbing you of the blessings of God. That old man is dead and gone, The New Birth is a reality ! **YOU ARE A NEW CREATION CREATED IN CHRIST JESUS !** Eternal life, the nature of God is at work in you. You do not have to wait until Heaven to enjoy your eternal life - you have it right now! It is yours!

REVELATION #3
REALITY OF BEING MADE THE RIGHTEOUSNESS OF GOD

When you become established in righteousness, you are on your way to victory! Righteousness is not something you can attain only after you get to Heaven. It is available now. **RIGHTEOUSNESS** is an Old English word that simply means **RIGHT- STANDING WITH GOD**. Second Corinthians 5:21 says, *He who knew no sin was made to be sin for us that we might be made the righteousness of God in Him*. You have been made the righteousness of God!

Romans 3:21-27 tells about this righteousness. Verse 22 says ...*the righteousness of God which is by faith of Jesus Christ unto all and upon all them that believe*... Someone might say, "But I thought the Bible says, There is none righteous, no, not one." Yes it does, but that was referring to man's own righteousness. Man's righteousness is as filthy rags, but Jesus has given us His righteousness. That is the story of the Gospel! Jesus was made sin

43

with our sinfulness so that we could become righteous with His righteousness.

You have right-standing with the God of the universe, and your right-standing with God gives you the ability to stand in the presence of Almighty God without a sense of sin, guilt, fear, inferiority, or condemnation. You have just as much right to stand before God as Jesus does. He purchased that right for you. You are enjoying His righteousness! Dwell on these things and allow them to become a reality in your inner man.

A revelation of being made the righteousness of God will cause your prayer life to become very accurate. The Bible says in I Peter 3:12, *For the eyes of the Lord are over the righteous, and his ears are open unto their prayers.*. James 5:16 says ..*The effectual fervent prayer of a righteous man availeth much*. The Amplified Bible reads this way: *The earnest (heartfelt, continued) prayer of a righteous man makes tremendous power available - dynamic in its working*. This is what the prayer of one righteous man will do. What do you suppose the prayer of two could do? Or ten? Or a hundred?

Get established in being made the righteousness of God and this kind of power will become operative in your prayer life. Whenever a crisis arises, you will know that the moment you pray, you get God's attention. When the force of righteousness is a working reality in your life, you will never be in a hurry, nor will you hesitate. Jesus was never in a hurry during His earthwalk. He always knew how every situation was going to turn out. Why? Because He was established in His righteousness, in His right-standing with the Father God. Psalm 37:25 says, ...*yet have I not seen the righteous forsaken, nor his seed begging bread.*

In many instances, the Amplified Bible uses the phrase UNCOMPROMISINGLY RIGHTEOUS. A person who is established in his right-standing with God will not compromise where the Word is concerned. Lean hard on your righteousness with God. Push it to its limits. You will see that Jesus, the Apostle and High Priest of your confession will back it with His power.

REVELATION #4
REALITY OF BEING GOD-INDWELT

There are three relationships between God and man revealed in the Bible:

1. God for us.
2. God with us.
3. God in us.

The Old Testament people were affected by only two of these relationships: God for them and God with them. You can see throughout the Old Testament that when the people had an assurance of these two relationships, they were guaranteed success.

Many times God spoke through the mouth of His prophets and said: *I AM THY GOD. I AM WITH THEE. I WILL NOT FORSAKE THEE.* Isaiah 41:10 says, *Fear thou not; for I am with thee: be not dis-*

mayed; for I am thy God: I will strengthen thee; yea, I will help thee; yea, I will uphold thee with the right hand of my righteousness.

When these Old Testament saints had an awareness of God being with them and for them, there was absolutely no defeat in their lives. What do you suppose they could have done having GOD IN THEM? The feats performed by God through Moses, Elijah, Samson, David, and all the rest were tremendous; but they were really nothing compared to the things every New Testament Believer should be accomplishing today. You are born of God. You have the mighty Holy Spirit dwelling in you. You are filled with God!

A revelation of being GOD-INDWELT will cause you to realize the fullness of your covenant with God. Second Corinthians 6:16 says, *I will dwell in them, and walk in them; and I will be their God, and they shall be my people.* You did not receive just a little dab of the Holy Ghost in your heart. YOU ARE WALL - TO- WALL HOLY GHOST ! The same

Holy Ghost that came on Samson and enabled him to slay 1,000 men with the jawbone of an ass; the same Holy Ghost that came on Elijah and caused him to outrun the Kings' chariots for twenty miles; the same Holy Ghost that split the Red Sea; the same Holy Ghost that took God's Word, *Let there be light!* and created 16 billion miles of universe; the SAME HOLY GHOST is living and dwelling and abiding INSIDE YOU! When this becomes a reality in your spirit, you will quote I John 4:4 with an assurance you have never known before. *GREATER IS HE THAT IS IN YOU THAN HE THAT IS IN THE WORLD.* This Scripture will be more than a cliche. It will mean something in your life.

When YOU walk, HE walks. When YOU stretch forth your hand, HE stretches forth His hand. No wonder the ministry of the laying on of hands is so vital in the life of a Christian! There is only one layer of skin between you and the Holy Ghost. Get established in the reality of being God-indwelt and you will not be afraid to lay hands on the sick. You will do so and expect them to recover that very moment. It is not your power that will bring the healing; it is the Greater One that dwells within you.

REVELATION #5
REALITY OF THE AUTHORITY
IN THE NAME OF JESUS

We have taken the Name of Jesus lightly in the past. We have repeated it without a true understanding of the power it contains. Philippians 2:9-11 tells us, *Wherefore God also hath highly exalted him, and given him a name which is above every name: That at the name of Jesus every knee should bow, of things in heaven, and things in earth, and things under the earth; And that every tongue should confess that Jesus Christ is Lord, to the glory of God the Father.*

No other name in the universe carries with it the power that the Name cf Jesus carries! God conferred power on the Name of Jesus and then He delegated the use of that Name to His Body. We are to take the Name of Jesus and govern circumstances,

demons, sickness, fear, and even hell itself! John 16:23 says, *And in that day ye*
shall ask me nothing. Verily, verily, I say
unto you, Whatsoever ye shall ask the Fa-
ther in my name, he will give it you. The
Name of Jesus will get the ear of God
quicker than anything you could ever say.
A man can have the nature of Satan residing in him and be bound straight for hell;
but he needs only to whisper the Name of
Jesus and the shackles of death will be
broken from him! There is power in the
Name of Jesus! How did His Name obtain such vast power and authority? Read
Hebrews 1:1-4:

God, who at sundry times and in divers
manners spake in time past unto the fa-
thers by the prophets, Hath in these last
days spoken unto us by his Son, whom he
hath appointed heir of all things, by whom
also he made the worlds: Who being the
brightness of his glory, and the express
image of his person, and upholding all
things by the word of his power, when he
had by himself purged our sins, sat down
on the right hand of the Majesty on high;

Being made so much better than the angels, as he hath by inheritance obtained a more excellent name than they.

The power in the Name of Jesus was received through inheritance. Jesus inherited His Name and the power it contains from the Father God. In order to find out how much power is vested in the Name of Jesus, you have to measure the power in God. How much power does the throne of God wield? There is no measuring stick large enough to tell! All the corporate structure of Heaven is backing the Name of Jesus. All God has and is and ever will be is in the Name of Jesus ! That is great, but it doesn't stop there. God has given the Name of Jesus to the body of Believers on earth. Our inheritance in Christ includes the ability and the right to use His Name to stop Satan. The forces of hell are subject to the Name of Jesus. THAT NAME CARRIES ALL POWER AND AUTHORITY - in heaven, in earth, and under the earth. Everything must bow to the Name of Jesus!

You have been given the power of attorney to use the Name just as if it were your very own. Would it change the way you are living now if you suddenly inherited the name of Rockefeller? If Mr. Rockefeller walked up to you and gave you the power of attorney to use his name anywhere on earth, would your position change in the world? Would that affect the way you are living today? Of course it would. Well, praise God, I want you to know that the name of Rockefeller will never see the day when it contains the power which the Name of Jesus carries - and HIS NAME HAS BEEN GIVEN FREELY TO YOU AND TO ME. Think about that!

REVELATION #6
REALITY OF THE INTEGRITY
OF GOD'S WORD

There is one important truth that must be established in your spirit if you ever expect to come to maturity in the Lord. That truth is this: GOD'S WORD IS HIS INTEGRITY, HIS BOND. Your Bible does not just contain the Word of God - it is the Word of God. When you think of the phrase GOD'S WORD, do you automatically visualize a black leather book? If you do, then you need to spend more time in the Word. When you think of a man's word, you automatically think of his integrity. IS HIS WORD GOOD? WILL HE DO WHAT HE SAYS? WILL HE BACK HIS WORD? This is how you should think of God's Word.

God's Word is His bond. He will do what He says. He will back His Word. In Jeremiah 1:12, God said, ...*I will hasten my word to perform it.* The Amplified Bible translates that verse like this: *For I am alert and active, watching over My word to perform it.* In Isaiah 55:11 God says, *So shall my word be that goeth forth out of my mouth: it shall not return unto me void, but it shall accomplish that which I please, and it shall prosper in the thing whereto I sent it.* According to Mark 16:20, God confirms His Word with signs following.

The Word of God is my Father's bond to me. Whenever He says something, I know He will back it with His actions. The best way to become truly aware of God's integrity is for you to develop your own integrity. You should be ready to back your word with actions. If you say you will be at a certain place at a certain time, make sure that you are there at that time. Be aware of the things you promise.

The Lord has pointed this out to me in my own life, particularly in dealings with my children. There were times when I would threaten to spank my daughters if they did something wrong. Then when they did it, I would only threaten them again. That had become my pattern of behavior until finally the Spirit of God rose up inside me and pointed out my error. You see, my children had realized that I would not back my word with actions. I would threaten them, but would never follow through. Consequently, they just overlooked my threats. Once I realized the situation, I was careful to back up my word to them.

This works the same way with God. You must realize that God has put out His

Word to us and He will back His Word with action. When this becomes a reality in your heart, your faith will become more highly developed. You will not be afraid to act on God's Word. He said it and He will see that it is carried out! HIS WORD IS HIS BOND TO YOU AND ME. It is a blood covenant between Almighty God and a man named Jesus Christ. When you make Jesus your Lord, then you become a partaker in that covenant. Whatever it says to Jesus is just as good for you and me. Let the reality of God's integrity become established in your spirit and you will not hesitate to act on God's Word. He will watch over His Word to perform it on your behalf.

REVELATION #'7
REALITY OF THE GOD KIND
OF FAITH RESIDING IN YOU

Ephesians 2:8, *For by grace are ye saved through faith; and that not of yourselves: it is the gift of God:* You received salvation through faith and the faith you used was provided for you by God. It was the gift of God.

Romans 12:3 tells us that God has dealt to every man *THE MEASURE OF FAITH*. The faith of God is in you - God put it there - and it will work for you.

The Apostle John wrote by inspiration of the Holy Ghost in I John 5:1,4, *Whosoever believeth that Jesus is the Christ is born of God...For whatsoever is born of God overcometh the world: and this is the victory that overcometh the world, even our faith.* The faith of Almighty God is in you and it will put you over! Jesus said in Mark 11:22, *Have faith in God* or *Have the God kind of faith.* When you make Jesus the Lord of your life, this God kind of faith is dealt to you. We learned previously in this study that we have been made partakers of God's divine nature, and His divine nature includes His faith.

You have faith, but your faith needs to be developed. This development will come only by the Word of God. Faith is created and fed by the Word. Romans 10:17 says, *So then faith cometh by hearing, and hearing by the Word of God.* Job said it very well this way: *I have not gone back from the commandments of His lips; I have esteemed and treasured up the words of His mouth* (Job 23:12 Amplified). Praise God! This God kind of faith IS residing in you and Jesus said, *All things are possible to him that believeth.* Are you a Believer? Then ALL things are possible unto you!

Become established in each of these seven major revelations from God's Word. When they become working revelations in your spirit, then your heart will be established and you will not be shaken over any situation. Whenever some crisis or pressure comes up before me, these revelations work as a checklist in my consciousness. I consider the situation or problem and apply these revelations to it in this manner:

HOW DOES THIS SITUATION AFFECT ME? I am redeemed by the blood of the Lamb.

HOW DOES THIS SITUATION AFFECT ME? I am a new creation, born of God. I have access to the ability of God

Himself. Therefore, I will reach into His wisdom and do the things He would do if He were faced with this problem.

HOW DOES THIS SITUATION AFFECT ME? I am the righteousness of God. Therefore, God's eyes are over me and His ears are open unto my prayers.

HOW DOES THIS SITUATION AFFECT ME? I have the God kind of faith residing in me. Jesus said that I could speak to a mountain and it would be removed; so I speak to this situation now, in the Name of Jesus, and command it to depart from me!

HOW DOES THIS SITUATION AFFECT ME? I have the power of attorney to use the Name of Jesus. Therefore, in the Name of Jesus, these circumstances must bow down before me.

HOW DOES THIS SITUATION AFFECT ME? I have a revelation of the integrity of my Father's Word. He is faithful that promised and His Word will not return unto Him void - it will accomplish that which He pleases and it will prosper in the thing whereto He sent it. Therefore, I will speak forth the Word of my Father and He will back it with His power.

HOW DOES THIS SITUATION AFFECT ME? I am God-indwelt. Greater is He that is in me than he that is in the world. Satan is completely defeated!

By the time I reach the end of this check-list, I am fully aware by the authority of God's Word that the situation is conquered. Allow all these truths from the Word to become real in your spirit and you will walk out of every situation a winner - VICTORIOUS in EVERY area of your life.

CHAPTER
3

Establishing
Your
HEART
Through
Meditating
GOD'S
WORD

❦ ❦ ❦

It is very important for you to realize the need of establishing your heart in God's Word; but it is even more important to know how to go about it. It would be ridiculous for me to tell you the importance of establishing your heart in the Word without then instructing you in how it is done.

There have been enormous amounts of money and effort spent teaching men how to establish and build up their physical bodies. Even more has been spent in developing and building up men's minds. The one area that has been almost totally ignored is the establishing and building up and exercising of the spirit man - the reborn man inside you. It should be of utmost importance to us that the human spirit be taught and trained and cultivated until it has gained the ascendancy over the mind and body. This is God's intention for the Body of Christ. The Believer today should be governing his body and his mind with the Word of God.

There is a method presented in God's Word whereby your heart can become established on God's Word and that method is meditation in the Word. MEDITATING THE WORD OF GOD IS THE KEY TO ESTABLISHING YOUR HEART. God told Joshua to meditate in the Word. Look at Joshua 1:8: *This book of the law shall not depart out of thy mouth; but thou shalt meditate therein day and night, that thou mayest observe to do according to all that is written therein: for then thou shalt make thy way prosperous, and then thou shalt have good success.* The Amplified Bible says, ...*and then you shall deal wisely and have good success.* Within this Scripture is God's formula for prosperity, success, and dealing wisely in all the affairs of life: TALK THE WORD; MEDITATE THE WORD; ACT ON THE WORD.

Meditating the Word causes God's Word to indwell you. It will cause your heart to become established, fixed, and settled. Consequently, you will not be moved by the circumstances and situations around you. Let's look at Psalm 1:1-3. *Blessed is the man that walketh not in the counsel of the ungodly...But his delight is in the law of the Lord; and in his law doth he meditate day and night. And he shall be like a tree planted by the rivers of water, that bringeth forth his fruit in his season; his leaf also shall not wither, and whatsoever he doeth shall prosper.* This man delights in the law of the Lord and he meditates it day and night. As a result, he is fruitful in every situation and he prospers in everything he sets his hand to. The Amplified Bible reads, *...and everything he does shall prosper (and come to maturity).*

How would you like every Christian endeavor you are involved in to prosper and come to full maturity? The key to this kind of success is meditation in God's Word day and night.

Meditation is more than just reading the Word. To meditate the Word literally means to FIX YOUR MIND ON THE WORD AND DWELL ON IT IN YOUR THOUGHT LIFE DAY AND NIGHT. You can meditate the Word while you are driving a car, buying groceries, washing dishes, or sitting at the dinner table.

I meditate the Word almost constantly. Many times while I travel between meetings, I dwell on certain Scriptures and just let them roll over and over in my thinking. By doing this, those Scriptures leave my head and get down in my heart. Then the Holy Ghost paints a picture inside me and I will begin to see myself in the light of that Word.

There are some things you need to know about preparation to meditate God's Word. As an example for you, I want to describe how I go about meditating the Word in my own life. The first thing I do is pray in the spirit. The Bible says that when you pray in an unknown tongue, your mind is unfruitful. This is my goal:

to get my mind in neutral. I pray in the spirit until I can get my mind to shut down; then I will be able to hear the voice of the Spirit of God.

Let me just say here that it is difficult to watch television for a couple of hours and then expect to immediately begin meditating the Word. You cannot make the switch effectively without some kind of preparation.

Once I have my mind quiet, I begin to read over the particular Scriptures I intend to meditate. I read them over and over and over until I have a mental picture of what it is saying. As this picture is formed in my mind, I put my Bible down and begin to dwell on it. If I have trouble getting a clear picture, I go back and read it again. After some time spent this way, that picture will become so vivid in your thinking that you can almost see the expressions on the faces. Those Scriptures will become so real to you that you will never forget them. They will actually become a part of you.

As the Holy Spirit paints a picture in my spirit, I just sit quietly, absorbing it and allowing that Word to absorb me. Then I purposely listen to the voice of the Spirit of God. You see, the Holy Spirit was on the scene when Jesus walked the earth. He was there at Pentecost. He was there during the Acts of the Apostles. He was the One Who inspired holy men to write these things on paper so that you and I could enjoy them and benefit from them today. The Holy Spirit was there and He fully understands what the Word is saying. The SAME Holy Spirit is within me so I say this to Him: "Holy Spirit, You were there when this took place. You were there causing these things to be performed. You are in me now so, in the Name of Jesus, I expect You to reveal to me the deep things of God." At this point, it is as if a movie screen is flipped on in my mind. I begin to visualize on that screen what the Word is saying; and the Holy Ghost begins to explain it to me step by step. As a result of that, I never forget His explanations - I never forget the things I learn this way.

This is how I became established in Philippians 4:19. I meditated on that Scripture until it became as much a part of me as my right arm. At that point in my life, I needed to know that God would meet my needs according to His riches in glory by Christ Jesus. The truth of that Scripture is in my heart today and you will never convince me that God will not meet my needs. When a financial need arises, I refuse to bow to it. I refuse to let go of my faith because my heart is established in Philippians 4:19. It is a reality inside me and I will not be moved or shaken.

One of the first things I learned from purposely meditating God's Word is found in Hebrews 4:12-16. The 14th and 16th verses are the ones I was particularly dwelling on. At that time, I was in need. I needed financial help desperately. The business debts I had incurred before I was saved were almost overwhelming; but I believed that God would meet my needs and help me out of that situation. While I was praying and believing God for a financial miracle, I began to mediate these Scriptures:

Seeing then that we have a great high priest, that is passed into the heavens, Jesus the Son of God, let us hold fast our profession. . .Let us therefore come boldly unto the throne of grace, that we may obtain mercy, and find grace to help in time of need.

We have a great high priest, Jesus Christ Who is seated at the right hand of God - a high priest that is touched with the feeling of our infirmities. In other words, He knows where you are and He knows what you need. You will never encounter anything in your life that Jesus has not already experienced. He knows what it is like to be under pressure, and He has given us His ability to overcome the situation and relieve the pressure.

As I was meditating and dwelling on these Scriptures, the Holy Ghost began to paint an image in my spirit. I saw myself literally going up to the throne of God. I walked up before Jesus as He was seated at the right hand of the Father. I stood before them and looked at them. I will never forget the compassion in Jesus' eyes. He desired to meet my every need. They were awaiting my petition. When I spoke, there was a boldness in me; I was without fear because I belonged there. I said, "Father, in the Name of Jesus, Mark 11:24 says that whatsoever I desire when I pray, believe I receive it, and I shall have it." I paused for a moment; and when no one spoke, I continued, "Father, Jesus said that in this day I would ask Him nothing, but whatever I would ask You in His Name, You would give it to me. Father, I believe Philippians 4:19 that You shall supply my need according to Your riches in glory by Christ Jesus." Then I stood back and watched them. I will never forget what Jesus did. He leaned over and nudged the Father with His elbow and whispered, " Give it to him ." Praise God! I knew then that my worries were over. I knew that I had free access to the throne of the Living God. Everything I had pictured was totally scriptural. The Bible says in Hebrews 7:25 that Jesus *EVER LIVETH TO MAKE INTERCESSION* for the saints. He interceded on my behalf and the petition was granted.

Whenever a financial need arises now, I am not shaken by it. I have my heart established because I took the time to meditate God's Word in this area. There are plenty of opportunities to be shaken, but I refuse to receive them. I just go to the throne and have a little talk with my Father and my Lord Jesus.

CHAPTER
4

*Holding
Fast
To The*
WORD

❧   ❧   ❧

The established heart trusts in the Word of God. It is not moved by contradictory evidence. It is moved only by what it believes and it believes the Word. When circumstances are contrary to the Word - when common sense is contrary to the Word - the established heart always leans to the Word and refuses to be troubled.

We have studied the importance of meditating the Word. Now I want us to turn our attention to the necessity of being a doer of the Word. God told Joshua to meditate in the Word day and night so that he would *DO ACCORDING TO ALL THAT IS WRITTEN THEREIN*. It is through meditation in the Word that we become doers of the Word. James 1:25 says that a doer of the Word will be blessed in his deed. The first chapter of James warns us about hearing the Word, but not doing it. It says that such a man has deceived himself. If you fail to act on the Word, then you really do not believe it. If you believe a man's word, you will act on it. BELIEVING DEMANDS ACTION.

Let's look at an example of this from Jesus' ministry. In Luke 17:12-19 we see the account of ten lepers who asked Jesus to cleanse them. Verse 12 says that these lepers *STOOD AFAR OFF*. Under Levitical law, it was unlawful for a leper to enter the village. If they did, they could be stoned. As they stood afar off, they called to Jesus and said, *Jesus, Master, have mercy on us*. Jesus answered them with something which in the natural was impossible. He said, *Go shew yourselves unto the priest*. If they went to the temple with leprosy, they would be stoned.

However, I want you to realize what Jesus was doing here. Under Levitical law, there was provision for a leper to be cleansed. Once he was clean, he had a legal right to enter the temple and show himself to the priest. The priest would then declare him clean and he was free to return to his village. Jesus knew the Levitical Law and He was speaking the end result to these lepers. He saw them completely healed and cleansed so He told them to act like it. If they had been only hearers of the Word, they would have said, "But, Jesus, you don't understand. We can't go to the priests. We have leprosy! " Apparently, these men did not argue with Jesus. They believed His Word and acted accordingly. The Bible says, *As they went, they were cleansed.*

Those ten lepers relied on the integrity and the power of Jesus' words. They believed it to the point that they would act on it without question. They acted on the Word without hesitation. James wrote that *Faith without works is dead* (James 2:20). One translation reads, *Faith without corresponding actions is void and destitute of power.* If you really believe, you will act. Once you get your actions corresponding with what you believe, then as James said, your faith will be made perfect.

Once you have spent time meditating God's Word and acting on what that Word says, there will come a time when you must hold fast to the Word. Many times we miss out on the blessings of God simply because we let go too soon. Circumstances may indicate that there is no way for you to overcome a particular situation; but you must not let go of the Word. Keep talking the Word. Keep holding fast to the confession of your faith.

Let us hold fast the profession of our faith without wavering; (for he is faithful that promised) ... Cast not away therefore your confidence, which hath great recompence of reward. For ye have need of patience, that, after ye have done the will of God, ye might receive the promise. (Hebrews 10:23, 35-36). Holding fast to the Word of God is literally the same as being patient. Patience means TO BE CONSTANT, CONSISTENT, NEVER CHANGING REGARDLESS OF THE CIRCUMSTANCES. When you are exercising patience, you will talk and act the same regardless of the situation.

78

CAST NOT AWAY THEREFORE YOUR CONFIDENCE. Don't cast aside your faith just because it looks as if it is not working in your particular situation. Hold fast to the confession of your faith. Hold fast to the Word.

James 1:2-4 says, ... *count it all joy when ye fall into divers temptations; Knowing this, that the trying of your faith worketh patience. But let patience have her perfect work, that ye may be perfect and entire, wanting nothing.* Suppose you are believing God for the answer to a particular problem. All the evidence presented by your five physical senses is proving that you will not receive your answer. You finally reach the point where you are ready to cast your faith aside and write it off as a bad deal. Don't do that. Don't cast away your faith. *HOLD FAST TO THE PROFESSION OF YOUR FAITH.* Don't waver.

You see, when it looks as if nothing is working, your faith is being tried. As James 1:3 says, ...*the trying of your faith worketh patience.* In other words, when your faith is being tried, it puts to work the force of patience. Faith and patience work hand in hand. They always work together. Patience is the spiritual force that supports and undergirds your faith, so that it will not be cast from one side to the other. When your faith is being tested, the force of patience comes into motion. Then instead of casting away your faith and talking contrary to what the Word says, you will be strengthened and reinforced by the force of patience so that you remain constant and stable.

PUT GOD'S WORD FIRST

Psalm 112 is God's picture of the Believer. The established heart becomes established and fixed as a result of putting God's Word FIRST PLACE and allowing the Word to be FIRST IN IMPORTANCE, above all else.

Once we get full of God's Word and allow the Word to establish our hearts, then our image and God's image will match. We will begin to see ourselves as God sees us.

80

God believes in the substitutionary sacrifice at Calvary. Because He believes it, He is not moved by what He sees and has seen through the last 2,000 years. He sees us through the redemptive work at Calvary. He sees us through the Blood of Jesus. I am convinced that the Father God sees us as a people with our hearts established and fixed, immovable.

It is time for the Body of Christ to match that image. It is time for Christians to leave the spiritual milk and get on the strong meat of the Word of God.

In this day and time, you cannot afford the luxury of not putting God's Word first place. The things happening these days will divide the men from the boys where the Gospel is concerned. It is our responsibility as Believers to become so established in God's Word that nothing shakes us, that we can stand boldly in the face of every situation and confess without a doubt, WE ARE MORE THAN CONQUERORS !

When you become established on God's Word, you become extremely dangerous to Satan. Through the Word, you can completely stop his operation in your own life, in your family, in your business, in your town, in your nation, and in the world! A person who is full of God's Word is a vehicle or a carrier of the power of the Almighty God. The creative ability of God is in His Word. No wonder Satan works so hard to get that Word out of your heart. You must be on guard and not allow him to be successful in his attempts to steal that Word. James wrote, *Resist the devil, and he will flee from you.*

Jesus was our example of how to resist Satan. He took the Word of God and said, *It is written...* Jesus was combating Satan with the two-edged sword of the Spirit - the Word of God. When Satan comes to steal the Word from you, take the Word and resist him with it. He MUST flee from you!

Make a quality decision to become established in the Word of God, to become strong in the power of the Lord. The moment you make that decision, there is nothing Satan and all of hell can do to stop it from coming to pass in your life!

Dr. Jerry Savelle is a noted author, evangelist, and teacher who travels extensively throughout the United States, Canada, and overseas. He is president of Jerry Savelle Ministries International, a ministry of many outreaches devoted to meeting the needs of believers all over the world.

Well-known for his balanced Biblical teaching, Dr. Savelle has conducted seminars, crusades and conventions for over twenty years as well as holding meetings in local churches and fellowships. He is being used to help bridge the gap between the traveling ministry and the local church. In these meetings, he is able to encourage and assist pastors in perfecting the saints for the work of the ministry. He is in great demand today because of his inspiring message of victory and faith and his accurate and entertaining illustrations from the Bible. He teaches the uncompromising Word of God with a power and an authority that is exciting, but with a love that delivers the message directly to the spirit man.

When Dr. Savelle was 12 years old, God spoke to his heart as he was watching the healing ministry of Oral Roberts on television. God told him that He was calling him into the ministry. Some years later, Dr. Savelle made Jesus Christ the Lord of his life and since that time has been moving in the light of that calling.

Dr. Savelle is the founder of Overcoming Faith Churches of Kenya, and the missions outreach of his ministry extends to over 50 different countries around the world. His ministry also delivers the powerful message of God's Word across the United States through the JSM Prison Ministry Outreach.

Dr. Savelle has authored a number of books and has an extensive cassette teaching tape ministry. Thousands of books, tapes, and videos are distributed around the world each year through Jerry Savelle Ministries.

For a complete list of tapes, books, and videos by Jerry Savelle, write:

Jerry Savelle Ministries
P. O. Box 748
Crowley, TX 76036

Feel free to include your prayer requests and comments when you write.